Destiny Diary

Destiny Diary

New Moon Guide
2011

Judith Pence Alderson
Carlyn Pence Krieger

Destiny Diary
New Moon Guide 2011

Cover Design: John Bigl
Interior Illustrations: John Bigl
www.bigldesign.com

ISBN: 978-0-615-38364-4

To order additional copies, please contact us:
Moon Wish Publishing
www.destinydiary.com
orders@destinydiary.com

New Moon Guide

2011

Destiny

The Destiny Diary was created with the hope of awakening people to their role in creating their own destiny and to obtain more control of their lives by being more aware of the cycles of nature. The most obvious and easiest cycle for all of us to observe is the daily cycle of the moon. To believe that we have some control over our lives is a belief that may come and go at different stages of our lives. When life seems to be stable we tend to believe that we are on the right path and living out our destiny, we feel that we have some control and life is good. There are times when situations change, life becomes chaotic and we are faced with circumstances that we could not even have imagined let alone manifested for ourselves.

The Destiny Diary was created with the belief that we are co-creators of our destiny, we are not able to do it alone. We need the help of nature, as well as divine guidance, in order to manifest what may be for our highest good. However, as with any partnership, we need to hold up our end of the bargain. Our end of the bargain is actually very small. The whole purpose of the Destiny Diary is to guide you through the steps of your part of the bargain in creating and manifesting your destiny.

On a subtle level we are all a part of the rhythms of nature which provide us with perfect timing and we need to be aware of that timing and use it to our benefit. When we use nature's cycles we can become gardeners planting at the right time knowing that plants will grow because nature's ways are very efficient. There is never doubt that seeds will grow; however, what has been planted still needs a certain amount of attention for the desired outcome. The purpose of the Destiny Diary is to provide a method to enhance the Laws of

Attraction and to confirm your intentions to bring forth the life you want and deserve.

There is a difference between a wish and a desire. A wish is a thought or fantasy with no direct action and never thought of as actually happening. A desire is much stronger backed with definite action to bring the desire into reality. The Destiny Diary uses the modern tools such as list making and goal setting along with the ancient wisdom of the moon cycles to take wishes, mold them into desires and make them more powerful and energized.

Writing down your desires and intentions is a way of taking wishes from your mind and putting them on paper in order to give them the energy needed to take root and grow. Focusing on your list of intentions at specific times of the moon increases the creative process that will bring about your desires. Some form of action every day is the fastest way to achieve what you desire such as affirmations, visualization, taking small steps toward a large goal.

We have designated the new moon as the most important time to put your desires out into the Universe but this is not our idea, the new moon has always been thought of as the time for successful new beginnings.

The Destiny Diary will help you to organize your efforts and guide you in realizing your destiny by using the cycles of nature. This realization does not always come easily and may need constant effort and attention on your part....but there will always be another new moon giving you another chance at the life you desire and deserve.

"A dreamer is one who can only find his way by moonlight, and his punishment is that he sees the dawn before the rest of the world."

-Oscar Wilde

Moon Cycles

The moon has been associated with emotions, intuition, feminine energy and creation. The new moon has long been known to be a time of new beginnings whether for planting, projects or self improvement.

The cycles of the moon have been the object of study and worship for thousands of years and used as a timing device for planting and harvesting crops. The moon cycles have been used by various cultures for rituals and the making of magic because it has always been recognized that something special happens on earth during these times. One complete cycle from new moon to new moon is 29.5 days.

Without the moon the earth would be in total chaos wobbling around without stability. It provides gravitational pull that keeps the earth spinning at just the right speed and just the right tilt so that we can all exist.

The moon has always been associated with the water element because of its role in creating the tides of the ocean. Gardeners know that during the new moon lunar gravity pulls the water up from the earth providing the fertile environment for the seeds to sprout. As the moonlight increases going into the first quarter phase, new growth is stimulated and by the full moon the seed has taken root and begun to grow. Light begins to diminish after the full moon and by the fourth quarter has decreased the gravitational pull making it a time to prune and weed.

The Destiny Diary uses the same cycle of the moon to grow the seeds of your desires and get you on the path of finding your true destiny. The moon travels through the twelve signs of the Zodiac (sections of the sky) during its 29.5 day journey around the Earth. The moon will spend 2-3 days in each astrological sign reflecting the energy of that sign coloring emotions and events happening at that time. We have given you the symbol and characteristic of each sign on the new moon pages and a brief overview of how that energy can be used to your benefit.

The moon is a major part of our lives and to understand ourselves we need to appreciate how the movement of the moon affects us. We are reminded daily of this ancient icon not only by looking up at the night's sky but also on weather broadcasts, newspapers, calendars and celebration of holidays. Looking up at the night sky during each moon phase is an excellent meditation and helps to open communication with your spiritual self.

Being aware of the rhythmic cycles of the moon can put you more in harmony with nature allowing you to create anything you desire. Writing in the Destiny Diary is the first step in becoming aware of the timing and cycles of the moon which can synchronize you with the universe.

How to Use the Destiny Diary

The Destiny Diary has been created to view an entire moon phase at a glance using the lunar week in an effort to help us become more aware of the moon cycles in our everyday life. The New Moon starts the first quarter of each cycle and two pages are devoted to this special day each month in preparation for the month ahead.

The day before each new moon your mind is open to possibilities. Be aware of your thoughts on this day and write down any ideas that could be helpful in creating your new moon list.

As you plant the seed of your intentions on the day of the new moon, water your intentions each day by reading over your list and journaling on a daily basis. Each thought you direct toward your desire is like a ray of sunlight helping it to grow. The more sunlight given to the seed of your intentions energizes them into blossoming into your life quickly and to grow stronger each day.

It is good to list some long term desires every month realizing that every month you are bringing your wishes closer to you and manifesting your desire.

The exact time when each quarter begins along with the zodiac sign is listed at the beginning of the quarter and includes a short explanation of the energy that may be prominent during that phase.

Daily journaling space is provided to use as a diary or as a planner. There is additional space at the end of each week to use for specific notes, "ah-ha" moments, or a To Do List.

There are quotes at the bottom of each page to help encourage you to stay motivated and not only to believe but expect miracles each day. Journaling your success is part of the process of creating your destiny.

The New Moon Pages

Each new moon page gives the exact time (Eastern Time) of the new moon and the sign of the Zodiac with information as to the best way to use the energy of the current new moon.

Writing down your desires within the first eight hours of the exact time of the new moon is the most powerful time, but within 24 hours is beneficial. The new moon page provides space to make a list of your desires. It is best to limit your list to no more than eight desires. This is the day to plant your intentions by listing your desires for the month both short and long term.

Listing desires for others does not seem to work. Desires must be for you alone because each person's path is unique and we are not able to determine another person's destiny.

When making your list be as specific as possible as you write down your desires. Visualize your desires coming true as you write them down.

Each day after the new moon you can journal your thoughts and activities. Look for evidence each day that your desires are coming to you. Expect circumstances to present themselves that will sprout the seeds of your desires. Expect miracles.

Days of the New and Full Moons

NEW MOON	FULL MOON
January 4	January 19
February 2	February 18
March 4	March 19
April 3	April 17
May 3	May 17
June 1	June 15
July 1	July 15
July 30	August 13
August 28	September 12
September 27	October 11
October 26	November 10
November 25	December 10
December 24	

Moon Phases

First Quarter

The new moon begins the first quarter and is called the "dark of the moon" because the moon appears to be invisible. The new moon crescent cannot actually be seen until 5-12 hours after the exact time of the new moon and can be seen as it rises and sets with the sun.

During the week following the new moon your motivation to achieve your desires remains at a high level and you optimistically embrace new beginnings. It is a time when your inner world is dominant making your dreams as well as your intuition very close to the surface.

This phase is the best time to be the observer of everyday happenings around you. You will be able to recognize subtle coincidences in your life that you would not recognize during other phases of the moon. Recognizing them will give you a chance to see the pattern of your destiny unfolding. Be sure to record these coincidences in your Diary.

Second Quarter

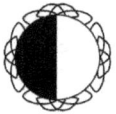

The moon is increasing in light or waxing and can be seen as it rises at noon and sets at midnight.

During this phase your outer world may seem more prominent and dominates your attention. This could be frustrating because you may not be able to give full attention to your desires due to other obligations and dealing with day to day challenges. You feel as if you need to put your intentions aside for what you perceive as the real world.

There are notes at the beginning of the second quarter pages that are meant to help you stay focused. This is the time when it would be very easy to lose track of what was important to you during the new moon and veer from the course of action to accomplish your goals. Review your list of desires and decide how you can get yourself back on track. As the full moon gets closer by the end of the week, you will feel more at ease.

Third Quarter

The full light of the moon starts the third quarter phase and can be seen rising in the east at sunset. This starts the "waning" period and the moon will start to decrease in light this week.

The day of the exact full moon generates a great deal of energy for everyone on the planet. It is an accumulation of everything that has been hidden for the last two weeks and can manifest as either positive or negative events.

The third quarter will provide the light to get a clearer vision of what needs to be done to accomplish your goals. During this phase you can see your obstacles clearly and take steps to minimize them in the next quarter.

Notes provided for the third quarter will aid you in visualizing your intentions and bringing them into the light of the full moon.

Fourth Quarter

The moon continues to decrease in light this week preparing for the new moon next week and can be seen in the eastern sky during the late evening hours. This is a time to weed out any negative thoughts or behaviors that might be preventing you from receiving your desires.

This quarter is similar to the second quarter in that everyday activities become more prominent and it seems as if your desires have to take a back seat.

As you become more in tune with the rhythmic cycles of the moon you'll find that going with the flow is your best tool for achieving your desires during the last quarter.

During the days of the last quarter resting and listening to your inner voice will allow you to envision the possibilities for the next new moon. By the end of the week you will be ready to reorganize your priorities and will be looking forward to the next new moon phase with enthusiasm.

Celestial Bookmarks

During a solar eclipse, the moon casts a shadow on the earth. During a lunar eclipse, the earth casts a shadow on the moon.

A **solar eclipse** is a very special New Moon. Between the time of the eclipse and the next full moon (about two weeks) seeds we plant, projects we undertake, contacts we make, and intentions we set, take on added significance in the next six months.

A **lunar eclipse** is also a very special Full Moon. Decisions we make, ideas we let go of, and things we finish during this waning cycle have added significance in the future.

If an eclipse falls on the same degree as a planet in your natal astrology chart the affairs of that house become more significant and generate more activity in the areas of your life associated with that house.

The two **solstices** and the two **equinoxes** mark the beginning of the four seasons. All traditions recognize the sun's journey as a potent power in the seasonal transitions symbolizing great change on the earth. Celebrations created to mark these events are seen as opportunities to give expression to and participate in a relationship to the cycles of nature.

New Moon Names

NEW MOON	NAME
January 4	Moon of Resolutions
February 2	Love Moon
March 4	Spring Forward Moon
April 3	Moon of Faith
May 3	Mother's Moon
June 1	Summer Moon
July 1	Patriotic Moon
July 30	Blue Moon
August 28	Stargazing Moon
September 27	Harvest Moon
October 26	Magic Moon
November 25	Moon of Gratitude
December 24	Giving Moon

**Throughout the ages various names have been given to the full moons. We have created names for each new moon based on what might be the collective consciousness of people during each month.

2011

JANUARY

S	M	T	W	T	F	S
						1
2	3	**4**	5	6	7	8
9	10	11	12	13	14	15
16	17	18	19	20	21	22
23	24	25	26	27	28	29
30	31					

FEBRUARY

S	M	T	W	T	F	S
		1	**2**	3	4	5
6	7	8	9	10	11	12
13	14	15	16	17	18	19
20	21	22	23	24	25	26
27	28					

MARCH

S	M	T	W	T	F	S
		1	2	3	**4**	5
6	7	8	9	10	11	12
13	14	15	16	17	18	19
20	21	22	23	24	25	26
27	28	29	30	31		

APRIL

S	M	T	W	T	F	S
					1	2
3	4	5	6	7	8	9
10	11	12	13	14	15	16
17	18	19	20	21	22	23
24	25	26	27	28	29	30

MAY

S	M	T	W	T	F	S
1	2	**3**	4	5	6	7
8	9	10	11	12	13	14
15	16	17	18	19	20	21
22	23	24	25	26	27	28
29	30	31				

JUNE

S	M	T	W	T	F	S
			1	2	3	4
5	6	7	8	9	10	11
12	13	14	15	16	17	18
19	20	21	22	23	24	25
26	27	28	29	30		

JULY

S	M	T	W	T	F	S
					1	2
3	4	5	6	7	8	9
10	11	12	13	14	15	16
17	18	19	20	21	22	23
24	25	26	27	28	29	**30**
31						

AUGUST

S	M	T	W	T	F	S
	1	2	3	4	5	6
7	8	9	10	11	12	13
14	15	16	17	18	19	20
21	22	23	24	25	26	27
28	29	30	31			

SEPTEMBER

S	M	T	W	T	F	S
				1	2	3
4	5	6	7	8	9	10
11	12	13	14	15	16	17
18	19	20	21	22	23	24
25	26	**27**	28	29	30	

OCTOBER

S	M	T	W	T	F	S
						1
2	3	4	5	6	7	8
9	10	11	12	13	14	15
16	17	18	19	20	21	22
23	24	25	**26**	27	28	29
30	31					

NOVEMBER

S	M	T	W	T	F	S
		1	2	3	4	5
6	7	8	9	10	11	12
13	14	15	16	17	18	19
20	21	22	23	24	**25**	26
27	28	29	30			

DECEMBER

S	M	T	W	T	F	S
				1	2	3
4	5	6	7	8	9	10
11	12	13	14	15	16	17
18	19	20	21	22	23	**24**
25	26	27	28	29	30	31

Hebrew Year 5771 Islamic Year 1432 Chinese Year 4709

December 2010

4th Quarter
11:20 pm in Libra

Relationships may be your focus this week.

Listening to the view of others can be beneficial.

DECEMBER						
S	M	T	W	T	F	S
			1	2	3	4
5	6	7	8	9	10	11
12	13	14	15	16	17	18
19	20	21	22	23	24	25
26	27	28	29	30	31	

28 Tue

29 Wed

30 Thu

31 Fri

Each day should be passed as though it were our last.

Publilius Syrus

January 2011 4th Quarter

JANUARY						
S	M	T	W	T	F	S
						1
2	3	4	5	6	7	8
9	10	11	12	13	14	15
16	17	18	19	20	21	22
23	24	25	26	27	28	29
30	31					

1 Sat **Happy New Year !!**

2 Sun

3 Mon **New Moon Tomorrow - Solar Eclipse**

Quarter Notes

The wise reject what they think, not what they see.

Huang-Po

January

Solar Eclipse

New Moon

4:04 am in Capricorn

This new moon would be good for tasks that take perseverance, discipline and organization and will provide the ability to accomplish more than you thought possible.

The symbol of Capricorn is a mountain goat sometimes with a dolphin's tail indicating that you have the ability to reach the top of the mountain even from the deepest places of the ocean.

Capricorn is a cardinal sign in the earth element with the energy to initiate change to get things done and at the same time being very practical giving attention to the details of individual daily needs.

List of Desires

4 Tue

4 Tue

To enjoy the world without judgment is what a realized life is like.
Charlotte Joko Beck

January

1st Quarter
4:04 am in Capricorn

JANUARY						
S	M	T	W	T	F	S
						1
2	3	4	5	6	7	8
9	10	11	12	13	14	15
16	17	18	19	20	21	22
23	24	25	26	27	28	29
30	31					

Resolutions New Moon

The new moon rises and sets with the sun.
Stay alert to coincidences this week.

5 Wed

6 Thu

7 Fri

8 Sat

You can't stop the waves but you can learn to surf.

Jack Kornfield

1st Quarter

9 Sun

10 Mon

11 Tue

Quarter Notes

The poor farmer makes weeds, the mediocre one makes crops, the skilled farmer makes soil.

Zen Saying

January

2nd Quarter

6:33 am in Aries

The second quarter is a time when it is easy to get off track from your original intentions made at the new moon.

Stay focused and review your list every day.

JANUARY						
S	M	T	W	T	F	S
						1
2	3	4	5	6	7	8
9	10	11	12	13	14	15
16	17	18	19	20	21	22
23	24	25	26	27	28	29
30	31					

12 Wed

13 Thu

14 Fri

15 Sat

There is no murder worse than killing time.

Yamamoto Gempo Roshi

2nd Quarter

16 Sun

17 Mon **Martin Luther King Day**

18 Tue

Quarter Notes

Dreams are like stars...you may never touch them, but if you follow them they will lead you to your destiny.

Anonymous

January

3rd Quarter
4:22 pm in Cancer

JANUARY						
S	M	T	W	T	F	S
						1
2	3	4	5	6	7	8
9	10	11	12	13	14	15
16	17	18	19	20	21	22
23	24	25	26	27	28	29
30	31					

Full Wolf Moon
The howling of the wolves is the loudest during this full moon because of hunger and the coldness of the season.

Let the full moon help you see
the path to your fulfillment.

19 Wed

20 Thu

21 Fri

22 Sat

It is in your moments of decision that your destiny is shaped.
Anthony Robbins

3rd Quarter

23 Sun

24 Mon

25 Tue

Quarter Notes

No trumpets sound when the important decisions of our life are made. Destiny is made known silently.

Agnes De Mille

January/February

4th Quarter
7:58 am in Scorpio

JANUARY						
S	M	T	W	T	F	S
						1
2	3	4	5	6	7	8
9	10	11	12	13	14	15
16	17	18	19	20	21	22
23	24	25	26	27	28	29
30	31					

Take time to look at any grudges held or resentments lingering and let them go in order to prepare for the next new moon.

26 Wed

27 Thu

28 Fri

29 Sat

In the realm of human destiny, the depth of man's questioning is more important than his answers.

Andre Malraux

4th Quarter

FEBRUARY						
S	M	T	W	T	F	S
		1	2	3	4	5
6	7	8	9	10	11	12
13	14	15	16	17	18	19
20	21	22	23	24	25	26
27	28					

30 Sun

31 Mon

February 1 Tues **New Moon Tomorrow**

Quarter Notes

Do not take life too seriously. You will never get out of it alive.
Elbert Hubbard

February

New Moon

9:32 pm in Aquarius

This is a good time to step outside of your usual routine and try something different that will show your unique individuality giving you the freedom to express yourself. Be open to new possibilities through friends and social gatherings.

The symbol of Aquarius is the water bearer and also known as the energy giver who shares his abundance with others.

Aquarius is a fixed sign in the air element showing that a focused mental outlook is unstoppable. It may appear that situations are erratic and uncertain but there is an undercurrent of purpose that will be dynamic when realized.

List of Desires

2 Wed

The destiny of man is in his own soul.

Herodotus

February

1st Quarter
9:32 pm in Aquarius

New Moon of Love

Pay attention to people and circumstances appearing unexpectedly with ideas.

FEBRUARY						
S	M	T	W	T	F	S
		1	2	3	4	5
6	7	8	9	10	11	12
13	14	15	16	17	18	19
20	21	22	23	24	25	26
27	28					

3 Thur **Chinese New Year of the Rabbit**

4 Fri

5 Sat

6 Sun

I know that I know nothing

Socrates

1st Quarter

7 Mon

8 Tue

9 Wed

10 Thu

Quarter Notes

The great end of life is not knowledge but action.

Thomas Henry Huxley

February

2nd Quarter
2:19 am in Taurus

Your mind may have trouble focusing on your intentions.

Gently bring your thoughts
back to where they were at the last new moon.

FEBRUARY						
S	M	T	W	T	F	S
		1	**2**	3	4	5
6	7	8	9	10	11	12
13	14	15	16	17	18	19
20	21	22	23	24	25	26
27	28					

11 Fri

12 Sat

13 Sun

14 Mon

There is no such thing as chance; and what seems to us merest accident springs from the deepest source of destiny.

Friedrich von Schiller

2nd Quarter

15 Tue

16 Wed

17 Thu

Quarter Notes

When I admire the wonder of a sunset or the beauty of the moon, my soul expands in worship of the Creator.

Mahatma Gandhi

February

3rd Quarter
3:37 am in Leo

Full Snow Moon
Also called Full Hunger Moon

Use the light to analyze your intentions.

FEBRUARY						
S	M	T	W	T	F	S
		1	2	3	4	5
6	7	8	9	10	11	12
13	14	15	16	17	18	19
20	21	22	23	24	25	26
27	28					

18 Fri

19 Sat

20 Sun

21 Mon **President's Day**

Becoming a star may not be your destiny, but being the best that you can be is a goal that you can set for yourself.

Bryan Lindsay

3rd Quarter

22 Tue

23 Wed

Quarter Notes

I'm not young enough to know everything.

J.M. Barrie

February/March

4th Quarter
6:27 pm in Sagittarius

FEBRUARY						
S	M	T	W	T	F	S
		1	2	3	4	5
6	7	8	9	10	11	12
13	14	15	16	17	18	19
20	21	22	23	24	25	26
27	28					

If you have travel plans this week, make sure you take your diary so you can write down all your insightful thoughts.

24 Thu

25 Fri

26 Sat

27 Sun

When your desires are strong enough you will appear to possess superhuman powers to achieve.

Napoleon Hill

4th Quarter

MARCH						
S	M	T	W	T	F	S
		1	2	3	**4**	5
6	7	8	9	10	11	12
13	14	15	16	17	18	19
20	21	22	23	24	25	26
27	28	29	30	31		

28 Mon

March 1 Tue

2 Wed

3 Thu **New Moon Tomorrow**

Quarter Notes

None will improve your lot, if you yourself do not.

Bertoft Brecht

March

New Moon

3:46 pm in Pisces

This is a time to be more aware of your inner life including dreams, imagination and intuition. These areas are sometimes hidden but are closer to the surface now where we can take advantage of any messages given to us in dreams, as well as daydreams.

The symbol of Pisces is two fish swimming in opposite directions explaining that sometimes it's good to look back so you can change your direction to reach your goal.

Pisces is a mutable sign in the water element meaning that emotions play a big part in decision-making so be prepared for decisions not to be permanent.

List of Desires

4 Fri

You control your future, your destiny. What you think about comes about. By recording your dreams and goals on paper you set in motion the process of becoming the person you most want to be. Put your future in good hands – your own.

Mark Victor Hansen

March

1st Quarter
3:46 pm in Pisces

Spring Forward New Moon

Write down any dreams or daydreams this week.

MARCH						
S	M	T	W	T	F	S
		1	2	3	4	5
6	7	8	9	10	11	12
13	14	15	16	17	18	19
20	21	22	23	24	25	26
27	28	29	30	31		

5 Sat

6 Sun

7 Mon

8 Tue

A goal without a plan is just a wish.

Antoine de Saint-Exupery

9 Wed **Ash Wednesday**

10 Thu

11 Fri

Quarter Notes

If you want to have a happy life, tie it to a goal, not to people or things.
Albert Einstein

March

2nd Quarter
6:46 pm in Gemini

Your home environment may temporarily demand your attention this week taking you off course.

Just make sure it is temporary and you get back to your new moon list soon.

MARCH						
S	M	T	W	T	F	S
		1	2	3	4	5
6	7	8	9	10	11	12
13	14	15	16	17	18	19
20	21	22	23	24	25	26
27	28	29	30	31		

12 Sat

13 Sun **Daylight Savings Time Begins**

14 Mon

15 Tue

You are important enough to ask and blessed enough to receive back.
Wayne Dryer

2nd Quarter

16 Wed

17 Thu **St. Patrick's Day**

18 Fri

Quarter Notes

Look deep into nature, and then you will understand everything better.
Albert Einstein

March

3rd Quarter
2:11 pm in Virgo

Full Worm Moon
The ground starts to become warm and earthworms appear.

Time to analyze, review and organize your list of desires.

MARCH						
S	M	T	W	T	F	S
		1	2	3	4	5
6	7	8	9	10	11	12
13	14	15	16	17	18	19
20	21	22	23	24	25	26
27	28	29	30	31		

19 Sat **Purim**

20 Sun **Vernal Equinox**
International Earth Day

21 Mon

22 Tue

Nothing is worth more than this day.

Goethe

3rd Quarter

23 Wed

24 Thu

25 Fri

Quarter Notes

Happiness is a continuation of happenings which are not resisted.
Deepak Chopra

March/April

4th Quarter
8:08 am in Capricorn

Your earthly duties may take priority now but you can work through them one step at a time.

MARCH						
S	M	T	W	T	F	S
		1	2	3	4	5
6	7	8	9	10	11	12
13	14	15	16	17	18	19
20	21	22	23	24	25	26
27	28	29	30	31		

26 Sat

27 Sun

28 Mon

29 Tue

A shot glass of desire is greater than a pitcher of talent.

Andy Munthe

4th Quarter

APRIL						
S	M	T	W	T	F	S
					1	2
3	4	5	6	7	8	9
10	11	12	13	14	15	16
17	18	19	20	21	22	23
24	25	26	27	28	29	30

30 Wed

31 Thu

April 1 Fri **National Walk to Work Day**

2 Sat **New Moon Tomorrow**

Quarter Notes

Why not go out on a limb? Isn't that where the fruit is?

Frank Scully

April

New Moon

10:33 am in Aries

This is the beginning of the astrological year and the time when energy is at its peak for starting new projects. Decide which of your desires will require high energy and enthusiasm because this is the time to get started.

The symbol of Aries is the ram with its head lowered and charging ahead not aware of any obstacles in its path.

Aries is a cardinal sign of the fire element meaning it is an initiator of action and will begin any task with the highest of energy.

List of Desires

3 Sun

Miracles happen every day. Not just in remote country villages or at holy sites halfway across the globe, but here, in our own lives.

Deepak Chopra

April

1st Quarter
10:33 am in Aries

Faith New Moon

Most religions have special holy days beginning with the spring equinox using the timing of the full moon and new moon.

APRIL						
S	M	T	W	T	F	S
					1	2
3	4	5	6	7	8	9
10	11	12	13	14	15	16
17	18	19	20	21	22	23
24	25	26	27	28	29	30

4 Mon

5 Tue

6 Wed

7 Thu

Those who dream by day are cognizant of many things which escape those who dream only a night.

Edgar Allen Poe

1st Quarter

8 Fri

9 Sat

10 Sun

Quarter Notes

Success is getting what you want. Happiness is wanting what you get.
Dale Carnegie

April

2nd Quarter
8:06 am in Cancer

You may want to relax and have fun this week, maybe use this time to be more creative and more specific about items on your new moon list.

APRIL						
S	M	T	W	T	F	S
					1	2
3	4	5	6	7	8	9
10	11	12	13	14	15	16
17	18	19	20	21	22	23
24	25	26	27	28	29	30

11 Mon

12 Tue

13 Wed **Day of Silence**

14 Thu

People with opinions just go around bothering one another.

Buddha

2nd Quarter

15 Fri

16 Sat

Quarter Notes

Goals are not only absolutely necessary to motivate us. They are essential to really keep us alive.
Robert H. Schuller

April

3rd Quarter
10:45 pm in Libra

APRIL						
S	M	T	W	T	F	S
					1	2
3	4	5	6	7	8	9
10	11	12	13	14	15	16
17	18	19	20	21	22	23
24	25	26	27	28	29	30

Full Pink Moon
Pink flowers bloom the earliest in spring.

Cooperation should be the theme of this week.

17 Sun

18 Mon

19 Tue **Passover**

20 Wed

Imagination is the beginning of creation. You imagine what you desire, you will what you imagine and at last you create what you will.

George Bernard Shaw

3rd Quarter

21 Thu

22 Fri **Earth Day**

23 Sat

Quarter Notes

Forever is composed of nows.

Emily Dickinson

April/May

4th Quarter
10:48 pm in Aquarius

APRIL						
S	M	T	W	T	F	S
					1	2
3	4	5	6	7	8	9
10	11	12	13	14	15	16
17	18	19	20	21	22	23
24	25	26	27	28	29	30

Enjoyment comes from being with special people or groups in your life

24 Sun **Easter**

25 Mon

26 Tue

27 Wed

Those who are awake live in a state of constant amazement.
Jack Kornfield

4th Quarter

MAY						
S	M	T	W	T	F	S
1	2	**3**	4	5	6	7
8	9	10	11	12	13	14
15	16	17	18	19	20	21
22	23	24	25	26	27	28
29	30	31				

28 Thu

29 Fri

30 Sat

May 1 Sun **May Day**

2 Mon **New Moon Tomorrow**

Quarter Notes

Talk does not cook rice.

Chinese proverb

May

New Moon

2:52 am in Taurus

Here is the time to list any desires for finances, material possessions or anything that holds value for you. Think of those things that provide contentment and security.

The symbol of Taurus is the bull, not charging but showing strength by being patient.

Taurus is a fixed sign in the earth element showing that fixity of purpose, or stubbornness, can be a virtue along with appreciation of the creature comforts of life.

List of Desires

3 Tue

Reduce your plan to writing. The moment you complete this, you will have definitely given concrete form to the intangible desire.

Napoleon Hill

May

1st Quarter
2:52 am in Taurus

Mother's New Moon

The moon represents the feminine energy necessary for creation.

MAY						
S	M	T	W	T	F	S
1	2	3	4	5	6	7
8	9	10	11	12	13	14
15	16	17	18	19	20	21
22	23	24	25	26	27	28
29	30	31				

4 Wed

5 Thu **Cinco de Mayo**

6 Fri

7 Sat

Man's task is to make himself a work of art.

Henry Miller

1st Quarter

8 Sun **Mother's Day**

9 Mon

Quarter Notes

The journey of a thousand miles begins with a single step.

Lao-tzu

May

2nd Quarter
4:34 pm in Leo

Don't worry if you are not on track this week. The intentions you made at the new moon are still working behind the scenes.

MAY						
S	M	T	W	T	F	S
1	2	3	4	5	6	7
8	9	10	11	12	13	14
15	16	17	18	19	20	21
22	23	24	25	26	27	28
29	30	31				

10 Tue

11 Wed

12 Thu

13 Fri

A consistent soul believes in destiny, a capricious one in chance.
Benjamin Disraefi

14 Sat

15 Sun

16 Mon

Quarter Notes

It isn't the great big pleasures that count the most; it's making a great deal out of the little ones.

Jean Webster

May

3rd Quarter
7:10 am in Scorpio

Full Flower Moon
Flowers become abundant now.

Look to nature to answer questions about the timing of important events.

MAY						
S	M	T	W	T	F	S
1	2	3	4	5	6	7
8	9	10	11	12	13	14
15	16	17	18	19	20	21
22	23	24	25	26	27	28
29	30	31				

17 Tue

18 Wed

19 Thu

20 Fri

People rarely succeed unless they have fun in what they are doing.
Dale Carnegie

3rd Quarter

21 Sat

22 Sun

23 Mon

Quarter Notes

The high destiny of the individual is to serve rather than to rule.
Albert Einstein

May

4th Quarter
2:53 pm in Pisces

Don't dwell on any perceived failures this month, realize they are part of the journey

MAY						
S	M	T	W	T	F	S
1	2	3	4	5	6	7
8	9	10	11	12	13	14
15	16	17	18	19	20	21
22	23	24	25	26	27	28
29	30	31				

24 Tue

25 Wed

26 Thu

27 Fri

No matter how qualified or deserving we are, we will never reach a better life until we can imagine it for ourselves and allow ourselves to have it.

Richard Bach

4th Quarter

28 Sat

29 Sun

30 Mon **Memorial Day**

31 Tue **New Moon Tomorrow – Solar Eclipse**

Quarter Notes

If enlightenment is not where you are standing, where will you look?
Zen Saying

June — New Moon

Solar Eclipse — **5:04 pm in Gemini**

The ability to communicate more effectively is the best way to use the energy of this new moon whether it be talking or writing. There is a lot of mental activity so ideas and thoughts are flowing quickly.

The symbol of Gemini is the twins, Castor and Pollux in Greek mythology, who in order to achieve their goal had to be able to understand each other completely.

Gemini is a mutable sign in the air element meaning that you could change your mind easily as your thoughts seem to come and go very quickly.

List of Desires

1 Wed

All that we are is the result of what we have thought. The mind is everything. What we think we become.

Buddha

June

1st Quarter
5:04 pm in Gemini

JUNE						
S	M	T	W	T	F	S
			1	2	3	4
5	6	7	8	9	10	11
12	13	14	15	16	17	18
19	20	21	22	23	24	25
26	27	28	29	30		

Summer New Moon

This is the week to beware of and write about your internal dialog.

2 Thu

3 Fri

4 Sat

5 Sun

Success is focusing the full power of all you are on what you have a burning desire to achieve.

Wilfred Peterson

1st Quarter

6 Mon

7 Tue

Quarter Notes

What you vividly imagine, ardently desire, sincerely believe, and enthusiastically act upon must inevitably come to pass.

Paul J. Meyer

June

2nd Quarter
10:12 pm in Virgo

JUNE						
S	M	T	W	T	F	S
			1	2	3	4
5	6	7	8	9	10	11
12	13	14	15	16	17	18
19	20	21	22	23	24	25
26	27	28	29	30		

When you get frustrated, maybe you are over analyzing.

Your desires will begin to unfold whether you analyze them or not.

8 Wed

9 Thu

10 Fri

11 Sat

Let the learner direct his own learning.

John Holt

12 Sun

13 Mon

14 Tue

Quarter Notes

Change your thoughts and you will change your world.
Norman Vincent Peale

June

3rd Quarter
4:15 pm in Sagittarius

Full Strawberry Moon
Also called Rose Moon

Let this quarter give you the light to see
how to overcome obstacles achieving your desires.

JUNE						
S	M	T	W	T	F	S
			1	2	3	4
5	6	7	8	9	10	11
12	13	14	15	16	17	18
19	20	21	22	23	24	25
26	27	28	29	30		

15 Wed **Lunar Eclipse**

16 Thu

17 Fri

18 Sat

When both body and mind are at peace, all things appear as they are: perfect, complete, lacking nothing.

Dogen

3rd Quarter

19 Sun **Father's Day**

20 Mon

21 Tue **Summer Solstice**

22 Wed

Quarter Notes

The choices we make and the chances we take, determine our destiny.

Unknown

June

4th Quarter
7:49 am in Aries

Do something for yourself this week, realize that being good to yourself benefits everyone.

JUNE						
S	M	T	W	T	F	S
			1	2	3	4
5	6	7	8	9	10	11
12	13	14	15	16	17	18
19	20	21	22	23	24	25
26	27	28	29	30		

23 Thu

24 Fri

25 Sat

26 Sun

Opportunity comes once in awhile, you got to see it, just like a shooting star.
Kazi Shams

4th Quarter

27 Mon

28 Tue

29 Wed

30 Thu **New Moon Tomorrow - Solar Eclipse**

Quarter Notes

Love thine enemies because they are the instruments to your destiny.
Joseph Campbell

July

Solar Eclipse

New Moon

4:55 am in Cancer

The energy of this new moon can be used for things pertaining to your home. Your feelings will be closer to the surface this month making you more sensitive than usual.

The symbol of Cancer is the crab that carries his home on his back so that he can retreat easily when threatened.

Cancer is a cardinal sign in the water element which makes this a fruitful time for planting the seeds of your desires, they will take root easily.

List of Desires

1 Fri

We are what we think. All that we are arises with our thought. With our thoughts, we make our world.

Buddha

July

1st Quarter
4:55 am in Cancer

Patriotic New Moon

Being a patriot is to show love, devotion and loyalty to your home, country and the world.

JULY						
S	M	T	W	T	F	S
					1	2
3	4	5	6	7	8	9
10	11	12	13	14	15	16
17	18	19	20	21	22	23
24	25	26	27	28	29	**30**
31						

2 Sat

3 Sun

4 Mon **Independence Day**

5 Tue

It is not in the stars to hold our destiny but in ourselves.

William Shakespeare

1st Quarter

6 Wed

7 Thu

Quarter Notes

The fruit of silence is tranquility.

Arabian Proverb

July

2nd Quarter
2:31 am in Libra

You may be trying to keep your life in balance this week. Keep your focus on the outcome you desire and the balance will happen.

JULY						
S	M	T	W	T	F	S
					1	2
3	4	5	6	7	8	9
10	11	12	13	14	15	16
17	18	19	20	21	22	23
24	25	26	27	28	29	30
31						

8 Fri

9 Sat

10 Sun

11 Mon

The world of reality has limits; the world of imagination is boundless.
Jacques Rousseau

2nd Quarter

12 Tue

13 Wed

14 Thu

Quarter Notes

If you wish to know the road up the mountain, you must ask the man who goes back and forth on it.

Zen Saying

July

3rd Quarter
2:41 am in Capricorn

Full Buck Moon
New antlers appear on buck deer.

You could see a new way to achievement
not noticed earlier.

JULY						
S	M	T	W	T	F	S
					1	2
3	4	5	6	7	8	9
10	11	12	13	14	15	16
17	18	19	20	21	22	23
24	25	26	27	28	29	30
31						

15 Fri

16 Sat

17 Sun

18 Mon

When you live your life with an appreciation of coincidences and their meanings, you connect with the underlying field of infinite possibilities.

Deepak Chopra

3rd Quarter

19 Tue

20 Wed

21 Thu

22 Fri

Quarter Notes

The secret to success is consistency of purpose.

Benjamin Disraeli

July

4th Quarter
1:03 am in Taurus

JULY						
S	M	T	W	T	F	S
					1	2
3	4	5	6	7	8	9
10	11	12	13	14	15	16
17	18	19	20	21	22	23
24	25	26	27	28	29	30
31						

Financial matters may be on your mind this week.

Nurture the mindset of abundance.

23 Sat

24 Sun

25 Mon

26 Tue

To accomplish great things, we must not only act, but also dream, not only plan, but also believe.

Amatole France

4th Quarter

27 Wed

28 Thu

29 Fri **New Moon Tomorrow**

Quarter Notes

If you care enough for a result, you will most certainly attain it.
William James

July

New Moon

2:41 pm in Leo

This is the time to think about what gives you joy and arrange to do more of it. Finding your passion and what gives you joy can help you to discover your destiny.

The symbol of Leo is the lion representing strength and leadership.

Leo is a fixed sign in the fire element which will provide the strength to endure obstacles and overcome them with enthusiasm making it enjoyable at the same time.

List of Desires

30 Sat

Our destiny changes with our thoughts; we shall become what we wish to become, do what we wish to do, when our habitual thought corresponds with our desire.
Orison Sweet Marden

July/August

1st Quarter
2:41 pm in Leo

Stargazing New Moon

Keeping your eyes on the stars and the meteor showers this month will keep you enthusiastic and inspired.

AUGUST						
S	M	T	W	T	F	S
	1	2	3	4	5	6
7	8	9	10	11	12	13
14	15	16	17	18	19	20
21	22	23	24	25	26	27
28	29	30	31			

31 Sun

August 1 Mon

2 Tue

3 Wed

Moon gazing makes me almost remember.

Judi Alderson

1st Quarter

4 Thu

5 Fri

Quarter Notes

Coincidences are spiritual puns.

G. K. Chesterton

August

2nd Quarter
7:09 am in Scorpio

Remain focused on your desires with the same intensity you had with the new moon.

AUGUST						
S	M	T	W	T	F	S
	1	2	3	4	5	6
7	8	9	10	11	12	13
14	15	16	17	18	19	20
21	22	23	24	25	26	27
28	29	30	31			

6 Sat

7 Sun

8 Mon

9 Tue

Only in solitude do we find ourselves.

Miguel De Unamuno

10 Wed

11 Thu

12 Fri **Perseids Meteor Shower**
Ramadan

Quarter Notes

We find no real satisfaction or happiness in life without obstacles to conquer and goals to achieve.

Maxwell Maltz

August

3rd Quarter
2:59 pm in Aquarius

Full Red Moon
Looks reddish when rising because of humid weather.

You may be able to see solutions through dreams and imagination.

AUGUST						
S	M	T	W	T	F	S
	1	2	3	4	5	6
7	8	9	10	11	12	13
14	15	16	17	18	19	20
21	22	23	24	25	26	27
28	29	30	31			

13 Sat

14 Sun

15 Mon

16 Tue

How refreshing, the whinny of a packhorse unloaded of everything!
Zen Saying

3rd Quarter

17 Wed

18 Thu

19 Fri

20 Sat

Quarter Notes

Somewhere, something incredible is waiting to be known.
Carl Sagan

August

4th Quarter
5:56 pm in Taurus

By talking to others, you sometimes are able to hear yourself solving your own problems

AUGUST						
S	M	T	W	T	F	S
	1	2	3	4	5	6
7	8	9	10	11	12	13
14	15	16	17	18	19	20
21	22	23	24	25	26	27
28	29	30	31			

21 Sun

22 Mon

23 Tue

24 Wed

Destiny, or karma, depends upon what the soul has done about what it has become aware of.
Edgar Cayce

4th Quarter

25 Thu

26 Fri

27 Sat **New Moon Tomorrow**

Quarter Notes

I like the silent church before the service begins, better than any preacher.
Ralph Waldo Emerson

August

New Moon
11:05 pm in Virgo

Now is the time to get organized and take care of tasks that require attention to detail. Take advantage of the mental clarity provided by this new moon to see how you can accomplish your desires.

The symbol of Virgo is a woman holding a shaft of wheat usually representing the time of harvest. The timing of the planting and the attention after planting will yield the best crops.

Virgo is a mutable sign in the earth element making it adaptable to most circumstances and using this flexibility to accomplish even the most tedious tasks.

List of Desires

28 Sun

Don't think-feel. It is like a finger pointing out to the moon, don't concentrate on the finger or you will miss all that heavenly glory.

Bruce Lee

August/September

1st Quarter
11:05 pm in Virgo

Harvest New Moon

Each day this week is another step closer to obtaining your goals.

AUGUST						
S	M	T	W	T	F	S
	1	2	3	4	5	6
7	8	9	10	11	12	13
14	15	16	17	18	19	20
21	22	23	24	25	26	27
28	29	30	31			

29 Mon

30 Tue

31 Wed

September 1 Thu

It's the constant and determined effort that breaks down all resistance and sweeps away all obstacles.

Claude M. Bristol

1st Quarter

SEPTEMBER						
S	M	T	W	T	F	S
				1	2	3
4	5	6	7	8	9	10
11	12	13	14	15	16	17
18	19	20	21	22	23	24
25	26	27	28	29	30	

2 *Fri*

3 Sat

Quarter Notes

A life spent making mistakes is not only more honorable, but more useful than a life spent doing nothing.

George Bernard Shaw

September

2nd Quarter
1:40 pm in Sagittarius

SEPTEMBER						
S	M	T	W	T	F	S
				1	2	3
4	5	6	7	8	9	10
11	12	13	14	15	16	17
18	19	20	21	22	23	24
25	26	**27**	28	29	30	

Your social calendar may be busier than usual this week, leave some time to review your list each day.

4 Sun

5 Mon **Labor Day**

6 Tue

7 Wed

One must not lose desires. They are mighty stimulants to creativeness, to love, and to long life.

Alexander A. Bogomoletz

8 Thu

9 Fri

10 Sat

11 Sun

Quarter Notes

The stars compel the soul to look upwards and lead us from this world to another.
Plato

September

3rd Quarter
5:28 am in Pisces

Full Harvest Moon
Most food for the winter ready to be harvested.

Appears to be one of the brightest moons showing the path to self discovery.

SEPTEMBER						
S	M	T	W	T	F	S
				1	2	3
4	5	6	7	8	9	10
11	12	13	14	15	16	17
18	19	20	21	22	23	24
25	26	**27**	28	29	30	

12 Mon

13 Tue

14 Wed

15 Thu

Nothing contributes so much to tranquilize the mind as a steady purpose-a point on which the soul may fix its intellectual eye.

Mary Wollstonecraft Shelley

3rd Quarter

16 Fri

17 Sat

18 Sun

19 Mon

Quarter Notes

The place you are right now God circled on a map for you.

Ibraham Hafiz

September

4th Quarter
9:40 am in Gemini

Is what you're feeling more real than what you're thinking?

SEPTEMBER						
S	M	T	W	T	F	S
				1	2	3
4	5	6	7	8	9	10
11	12	13	14	15	16	17
18	19	20	21	22	23	24
25	26	27	28	29	30	

20 Tues

21 Wed **International Day of Peace**

22 Thu

23 Fri **Autumn Equinox**

Would that life were like the shadow cast by a well or a tree, but it is like the shadow of a bird in flight.

Haggadah

4th Quarter

24 Sat

25 Sun

26 Mon **New Moon Tomorrow**

Quarter Notes

Dwell not upon thy weariness, thy strength shall be according to the measure of thy desire.

Arab proverb

September

New Moon

7:10 am in Libra

The new moon in Libra can be a good time to look at the harmony and balance in your life - balancing family, friends, partners, work, and pleasure.

The symbol of Libra is the scale of justice to be a reminder that everything must remain in balance to achieve harmony.

Libra is a cardinal sign in the air element indicating there is energy for accomplishing your desires by using your negotiating skills in relationships which can be very beneficial now.

List of Desires

27 Tue

We have to understand that the world can only be grasped by action, not by contemplation. The hand is more important than the eye... the hand is the cutting edge of the mind.

Jacob Bronowski

September/October

1st Quarter
7:10 am in Libra

SEPTEMBER						
S	M	T	W	T	F	S
				1	2	3
4	5	6	7	8	9	10
11	12	13	14	15	16	17
18	19	20	21	22	23	24
25	26	27	28	29	30	

Magic New Moon

Magical moments are available to you always and you just need to be open to them, especially this month.

28 Wed **Rosh Hashanah**

29 Thu

30 Fri

October 1 Sat **International Day for the Elderly**

I am enough of an artist to draw freely upon my imagination. Imagination is more important than knowledge. Knowledge is limited. Imagination encircles the world.

Albert Einstein

1st Quarter

OCTOBER						
S	M	T	W	T	F	S
						1
2	3	4	5	6	7	8
9	10	11	12	13	14	15
16	17	18	19	20	21	22
23	24	25	**26**	27	28	29
30	31					

2 Sun

Quarter Notes

I don't know what your destiny will be, but one thing I know; the only ones among you who will be really happy are those who have sought and found how to serve.

Albert Schweitzer

October

2nd Quarter
11:16 pm in Capricorn

Not much can distract you now, you're on an uphill climb.

OCTOBER						
S	M	T	W	T	F	S
						1
2	3	4	5	6	7	8
9	10	11	12	13	14	15
16	17	18	19	20	21	22
23	24	25	**26**	27	28	29
30	31					

3 Mon

4 Tue

5 Wed

6 Thu

You are here to enable the divine purpose of the universe to unfold. That is how important you are.

Eckhart Tolle

2nd Quarter

7 Fri Yom Kippur

8 Sat

9 Sun

10 Mon

Quarter Notes

Change in all things is sweet.

Aristotle

October

3rd Quarter
10:07 pm in Aries

OCTOBER						
S	M	T	W	T	F	S
						1
2	3	4	5	6	7	8
9	10	11	12	13	14	15
16	17	18	19	20	21	22
23	24	25	**26**	27	28	29
30	31					

Full Hunter's Moon
Leaves falling make it easier to see to hunt.

You can visualize your success easily now

11 Tue

12 Wed

13 Thu

14 Fri

Three things cannot be hidden: the sun, the moon and the Truth.
The Buddha

3rd Quarter

15 Sat

16 Sun

17 Mon

18 Tue

Quarter Notes

On whose door does the moonlight not shine?

Zen saying

October

4th Quarter
11:31 pm in Cancer

What do you absolutely love to do and can you do more of it?

OCTOBER						
S	M	T	W	T	F	S
						1
2	3	4	5	6	7	8
9	10	11	12	13	14	15
16	17	18	19	20	21	22
23	24	25	**26**	27	28	29
30	31					

19 Wed

20 Thu

21 Fri

22 Sat

You will always exist in the universe in one form or another.
Shunryu Suzuki

4th Quarter

23 Sun

24 Mon

25 Tue

Quarter Notes

Ignorance is the night of the mind, a night without moon or star.

Confucius

October

New Moon

3:57 pm in Scorpio

The energy of the Scorpio new moon is intense and full of secret powers coming from your intuitive nature. Trust your inner guidance this month and list desires that are for your highest good.

The symbol of Scorpio is the phoenix arising again out of its own ashes showing you can renew yourself if you have the burning desire to do so.

Scorpio is a fixed sign in the water element showing you can remain fixed in your purpose but emotions run deep and are closer to the surface than usual.

List of Desires

26 Wed

Through forgiveness, which essentially means recognizing the insubstantiality of the past and allowing the present moment to be as it is, the miracle of transformation happens not only within but also without.

Eckhart Tolle

October/November

1st Quarter
3:57 pm in Scorpio

New Moon of Gratitude

Taking time to be thankful will draw even more things to be thankful for.

OCTOBER						
S	M	T	W	T	F	S
						1
2	3	4	5	6	7	8
9	10	11	12	13	14	15
16	17	18	19	20	21	22
23	24	25	**26**	27	28	29
30	31					

27 Thu

28 Fri

29 Sat

30 Sun

The spirit and determination of the people to chart their own destiny is the greatest power for good in human affairs.

Matt Blunt

1st Quarter

NOVEMBER						
S	M	T	W	T	F	S
		1	2	3	4	5
6	7	8	9	10	11	12
13	14	15	16	17	18	19
20	21	22	23	24	25	26
27	28	29	30			

31 Mon **Halloween**

November 1 Tue **All Saints Day**

Quarter Notes

When your talents and the needs of the world cross, there lies your calling.
Aristotle

November

2nd Quarter
12:39 pm in Aquarius

NOVEMBER						
S	M	T	W	T	F	S
		1	2	3	4	5
6	7	8	9	10	11	12
13	14	15	16	17	18	19
20	21	22	23	24	**25**	26
27	28	29	30			

Your focus may be more on friends this week
And they may be able to give you insights into
your goals, hopes and wishes.

2 Wed **All Souls Day**

3 Thu

4 Fri

5 Sat

One day's exposure to mountains is better than cartloads of books.
John Muir

6 Sun **Daylight Savings Time Ends**

7 Mon

8 Tue **Election Day**

9 Wed

Quarter Notes

Think enough and you won't know anything.

Kenneth Patchen

November

3rd Quarter
3:17 pm in Taurus

NOVEMBER						
S	M	T	W	T	F	S
		1	2	3	4	5
6	7	8	9	10	11	12
13	14	15	16	17	18	19
20	21	22	23	24	**25**	26
27	28	29	30			

Full Beaver Moon
Beavers are busy preparing for winter before water becomes frozen.

Start preparing for your desires to become reality.

10 Thu

11 Fri

12 Sat

13 Sun

In the midst of movement and chaos, keep stillness inside of you.
Deepak Chopra

3rd Quarter

14 Mon

15 Tue

16 Wed

17 Thu

Quarter Notes

Life is what one wants in one's soul.

D.H. Lawrence

November

4th Quarter
10:10 am in Leo

Time to reflect and reorganize this week in preparation for a new beginning next week.

NOVEMBER						
S	M	T	W	T	F	S
		1	2	3	4	5
6	7	8	9	10	11	12
13	14	15	16	17	18	19
20	21	22	23	24	**25**	26
27	28	29	30			

18 Fri

19 Sat

20 Sun

21 Mon

The poor long for riches, the rich long for heaven, but the wise long for a state of tranquility.

Swami Rama

4th Quarter

22 Tue

23 Wed

24 Thu **Thanksgiving Day** **New Moon Tomorrow**
Solar Eclipse

Quarter Notes

The greatest thing in the world is to know how to be one's own self.
Montaigne

November

Solar Eclipse

New Moon

1:11 am in Sagittarius

This is an optimistic, lighthearted, fun new moon and good for creating social events that will be successful. It is also charged with spiritual energy helping with self awareness, self realization and study.

The symbol of Sagittarius is a centaur with the human portion drawing a bow and arrow targeted upwards with the enthusiasm of an excellent hunter.

Sagittarius is a mutable sign in the fire element showing that going with the flow may achieve more than adhering to routines now.

List of Desires

25 Fri

There is a perfect time for everything and that by flowing with these cycles (moon), life becomes easier.

Nanna

November/December

1st Quarter
1:11 am in Sagittarius

NOVEMBER						
S	M	T	W	T	F	S
		1	2	3	4	5
6	7	8	9	10	11	12
13	14	15	16	17	18	19
20	21	22	23	24	**25**	26
27	28	29	30			

New Moon of Giving

Sharing a positive outlook is the best gift ever.

26 Sat

27 Sun

28 Mon

29 Tue

The art of being wise is the art of knowing what to overlook.

William James

1st Quarter

DECEMBER						
S	M	T	W	T	F	S
				1	2	3
4	5	6	7	8	9	10
11	12	13	14	15	16	17
18	19	20	21	22	23	**24**
25	26	27	28	29	30	31

30 Wed

December 1 Thu

Quarter Notes

We are cups, constantly and quietly being filled. The trick is, knowing how to tip ourselves over and let the beautiful stuff out.

Ray Bradbury

December

2nd Quarter

4:53 am in Pisces

If you have low energy this week, relax and meditate on the best direction to go to achieve your goals.

DECEMBER						
S	M	T	W	T	F	S
				1	2	3
4	5	6	7	8	9	10
11	12	13	14	15	16	17
18	19	20	21	22	23	**24**
25	26	27	28	29	30	31

2 Fri

3 Sat

4 Sun

5 Mon

For others to approve of me is easy, for me to approve of myself is hard.
Yuan-Cheng

6 Tue

7 Wed

8 Thu

9 Fri

Quarter Notes

Traveler, there is no path. You make your path as you travel.
Antonio Machado

December

3rd Quarter
9:37 am in Gemini

Full Long Nights Moon
Midwinter nights are the longest.

Visualize your dreams coming true.

DECEMBER						
S	M	T	W	T	F	S
				1	2	3
4	5	6	7	8	9	10
11	12	13	14	15	16	17
18	19	20	21	22	23	**24**
25	26	27	28	29	30	31

10 Sat **Lunar Eclipse**

11 Sun

12 Mon

13 Tue **Geminids Meteor Shower**

A vigorous five mile walk will do more good for an unhappy but otherwise healthy adult than all the medicine and psychology in the world.

Paul Dudley White, MD

3rd Quarter

14 Wed

15 Thu

16 Fri

Quarter Notes

The Creator has not given you a longing to do what you have no ability to do.
Orison Swett Marden

December

4th Quarter
7:49 pm in Virgo

When nature is in balance, abundance and beauty are the result.

DECEMBER						
S	M	T	W	T	F	S
				1	2	3
4	5	6	7	8	9	10
11	12	13	14	15	16	17
18	19	20	21	22	23	**24**
25	26	27	28	29	30	31

17 Sat

18 Sun

19 Mon

20 Tue **Hanukkah**

Abundance is not something we acquire. It is something we tune into.
Wayne Dyer

4th Quarter

21 Wed

22 Thu

23 Fri **New Moon Tomorrow**

Quarter Notes

By three methods may we learn wisdom: First, by reflection, which is noblest; second by imitation, which is easiest; and third, by experience, which is the bitterest.

Confucius

December

New Moon

1:08 pm in Capricorn

This new moon is the time to get serious about what you want to accomplish for yourself in the coming year. You have the power and strength of Capricorn to make it happen.

The symbol of Capricorn is the mountain goat that may stumble on the way up the mountain but knows that is only part of the journey.

Capricorn is a cardinal sign in the earth element showing that efforts will be rewarded because the seeds planted now will have strong roots and be productive.

Our desire is that all your desires have been planted, nurtured and will grow into a prosperous and happy 2012.

List of Desires

24 Sat

What is life? It is the flash of a firefly in the night. It is the breath of a buffalo in the wintertime. It is the little shadow which runs across the grass and loses itself in the sun.

Crowfoot

December

1st Quarter

1:08 pm in Capricorn

Resolutions New Moon

The new moon rises and sets with the sun.
Stay alert to coincidences this week.

DECEMBER						
S	M	T	W	T	F	S
				1	2	3
4	5	6	7	8	9	10
11	12	13	14	15	16	17
18	19	20	21	22	23	**24**
25	26	27	28	29	30	31

25 Sun **Christmas Day**

26 Mon

27 Tue

28 Wed

Before you can score you must first have a goal.

Greek proverb

1st Quarter

29 Thu

30 Fri

31 Sat

Quarter Notes

Learn to be calm and you will always be happy.

ParamhansanYogananda

January 2012

2nd Quarter
1:16 am in Aries

The second quarter is a time when it is easy to get off track from your original intentions made at the new moon.

Stay focused and review your list every day

JANUARY						
S	M	T	W	T	F	S
1	2	3	4	5	6	7
8	9	10	11	12	13	14
15	16	17	18	19	20	21
22	23	24	25	26	27	28
29	30	31				

1 Sun **Happy New Year!**

2 Mon

3 Tue

4 Wed

Out beyond ideas of wrongdoing and rightdoing there is a field. I'll meet you there.
Rumi

5 Thu

6 Fri

7 Sat

8 Sun

Quarter Notes

Losing an illusion makes you wiser than finding a truth.

Ludwig Borne

2012

JANUARY

S	M	T	W	T	F	S
1	2	3	4	5	6	7
8	9	10	11	12	13	14
15	16	17	18	19	20	21
23	24	25	26	27	28	29
30	31					

FEBRUARY

S	M	T	W	T	F	S
			1	2	3	4
5	6	7	8	9	10	11
12	13	14	15	16	17	18
19	20	21	22	23	24	25
26	27	28	29			

MARCH

S	M	T	W	T	F	S
				1	2	3
4	5	6	7	8	9	10
11	12	13	14	15	16	17
18	19	20	21	22	23	24
25	26	27	28	29	30	31

APRIL

S	M	T	W	T	F	S
1	2	3	4	5	6	7
8	9	10	11	12	13	14
15	16	17	18	19	20	21
22	23	24	25	26	27	28
29	30					

MAY

S	M	T	W	T	F	S
		1	2	3	4	5
6	7	8	9	10	11	12
13	14	15	16	17	18	19
20	21	22	23	24	25	26
27	28	29	30	31		

JUNE

S	M	T	W	T	F	S
					1	2
3	4	5	6	7	8	9
10	11	12	13	14	15	16
17	18	19	20	21	22	23
24	25	26	27	28	29	30

JULY

S	M	T	W	T	F	S
1	2	3	4	5	6	7
8	9	10	11	12	13	14
15	16	17	18	19	20	21
22	23	24	25	26	27	28
29	30	31				

AUGUST

S	M	T	W	T	F	S
			1	2	3	4
5	6	7	8	9	10	11
12	13	14	15	16	17	18
19	20	21	22	23	24	25
26	27	28	29	30	31	

SEPTEMBER

S	M	T	W	T	F	S
						1
2	3	4	5	6	7	8
9	10	11	12	13	14	15
16	17	18	19	20	21	22
23	24	25	26	27	28	29
30						

OCTOBER

S	M	T	W	T	F	S
	1	2	3	4	5	6
7	8	9	10	11	12	13
14	15	16	17	18	19	20
21	22	23	24	25	26	27
28	29	30	31			

NOVEMBER

S	M	T	W	T	F	S
				1	2	3
4	5	6	7	8	9	10
11	12	13	14	15	16	17
18	19	20	21	22	23	24
25	26	27	28	29	30	

DECEMBER

S	M	T	W	T	F	S
						1
2	3	4	5	6	7	8
9	10	11	12	13	14	15
16	17	18	19	20	21	22
23	24	25	26	27	28	29
30	31					

Gratitude List for 2011

Reflections of 2011

Looking back over your new moon lists will give you insight into your unique cycles during the year. Each year as you use the Destiny Diary you will see a trend in your thought processes.

This self awareness will be a tool that will help you realize your own personal ebb and flow and how to use it to your advantage. Looking back also reinforces the wins you have had from your new moon goals.

Desires and Goals Accomplished

January

February

March

April

May

June

July

August

September

October

November

December

Visions for 2012

Plans and Goals for 2012

Destiny Contacts

Name ____
Home Phone_____________Cell_________________________
Email________________________Birthday_______________

Name ____
Home Phone_____________Cell_________________________
Email________________________Birthday_______________

Name ____
Home Phone_____________Cell_________________________
Email________________________Birthday_______________

Name ____
Home Phone_____________Cell_________________________
Email________________________Birthday_______________

Name ____
Home Phone_____________Cell_________________________
Email________________________Birthday_______________

Name ____
Home Phone_____________Cell_________________________
Email________________________Birthday_______________

Destiny Contacts

Name ____
Home Phone____________Cell________________________
Email_______________________Birthday______________

Name ____
Home Phone____________Cell________________________
Email_______________________Birthday______________

Name ____
Home Phone____________Cell________________________
Email_______________________Birthday______________

Name ____
Home Phone____________Cell________________________
Email_______________________Birthday______________

Name ____
Home Phone____________Cell________________________
Email_______________________Birthday______________

Name ____
Home Phone____________Cell________________________
Email_______________________Birthday______________

Business Contacts

Name ____
Home Phone____________Cell______________________
Email______________________Birthday_______________

Name ____
Home Phone____________Cell______________________
Email______________________Birthday_______________

Name ____
Home Phone____________Cell______________________
Email______________________Birthday_______________

Name ____
Home Phone____________Cell______________________
Email______________________Birthday_______________

Name ____
Home Phone____________Cell______________________
Email______________________Birthday_______________

Name ____
Home Phone____________Cell______________________
Eail______________________Birthday_______________

Business Contacts

Name ____
Home Phone ______________ Cell ___________________________
Email ___________________________ Birthday _________________

Name ____
Home Phone ______________ Cell ___________________________
Email ___________________________ Birthday _________________

Name ____
Home Phone ______________ Cell ___________________________
Email ___________________________ Birthday _________________

Name ____
Home Phone ______________ Cell ___________________________
Email ___________________________ Birthday _________________

Name ____
Home Phone ______________ Cell ___________________________
Email ___________________________ Birthday _________________

Name ____
Home Phone ______________ Cell ___________________________
Email ___________________________ Birthday _________________

Important Info

Passwords and Other Secrets

Birth Data

Sun Sign______________________________

Moon Sign _____________________________

Rising Sign____________________________

*If you do not have this information, contact us with your date, time and place of birth at chart@destinydiary.com and we will send it to you as a thank you for using the Destiny Diary.

Date of Birth___________________________

Time of Birth __________________________

Place of Birth__________________________

Favorite Websites

Thoughts

Insights

Notes and Doodles

Note from the Authors

If you have found this book, we hope that it has been of some help in your journey. Our hope is that 2011 has proven to be an insightful and rewarding year for you. Our intent in creating the Destiny Diary is to spark the awareness that you can play an important role in creating your destiny.

This realization provides the hope that you can have the successful and happy life you deserve. If you have begun to understand your unique purpose in life and have moved forward in fulfilling your destiny, we have accomplished our purpose.

You can also subscribe to the Destiny Diary NewMooners Newsletter which is emailed each month as a reminder of the new moon and provides more details on the astrological signs and their influences. To subscribe to the free Newsletter, contact us at newmooners@destinydiary.com.

Judith Pence Alderson
Carlyn Pence Krieger

Visit us online
www.destinydiary.com

www.ingramcontent.com/pod-product-compliance
Lightning Source LLC
Chambersburg PA
CBHW060829050426
42453CB00008B/630
* 9 7 8 0 6 1 5 3 8 3 6 4 4 *